The Legacy

I Talk You Talk Press

Copyright © 2018 I Talk You Talk Press

ISBN: 978-4-907056-96-4

www.italkyoutalk.com

info@italkyoutalk.com

All rights reserved. No part of this publication may be resold, reproduced, stored in retrieval system, copied in any form or by any means, electronic, mechanical, photocopying, recording or otherwise transmitted without the prior written permission from the publisher. You must not circulate this publication in any format, online or otherwise.

This is a work of fiction. Names, characters, businesses, organizations, products, places, events and incidents are either the products of the author's imagination or are used in a fictitious manner. We have no affiliation with any existing companies mentioned in this story. Any resemblance to actual persons, living or dead, existing stories or actual events is purely coincidental.

Although the author and publisher have made every effort to ensure that the contents of this book were correct at press time, the author and publisher do not assume and hereby disclaim any liability to any party for any loss, damage, or disruption caused by errors or omissions, whether such errors or omissions result from negligence, accident, or any other cause.

For more information, see the Copyright Notice on our website.

Image copyright: © Syda Productions - Fotolia.com #60287136 Standard license

CONTENTS

1. A new flatmate	1
2. A cold wet day	4
3. The letter	7
4. What are you doing?	8
5. Beth's mother	9
6. A very busy week	12
7. Silas	16
8. Margot has an idea	19
9. Brisbane Airport	21
10. Flight to Christchurch	24
11. Arriving in Christchurch	26
12. Great-Uncle William's house	30
13. Silas in New Zealand	33

14. The lawyer	35
15. Tim Gaskell	38
16. Who's been here?	42
17. Sightseeing	43
18. Silas feels lucky	47
19. A mystery	49
20. Confession	52
21. What shall we do?	55
22. No luck	58
23. Where is the painting?	60
24. The next day	66
25. Tim talks to the boss	70
26. We are looking for the thief	72
27. Wellington	77
Thank You	80
About the Author	81

1. A NEW FLATMATE

Beth Whitley-Sneddon lived in a flat about 3km from the centre of Manchester. She shared the flat with her best friend Penny Green. Beth was a secretary for the manager of a big department store in the centre of Manchester. Penny worked for an insurance company.

Beth was tall and slim. She had long silvery blonde hair and green eyes. Penny was small and round with shiny black hair and big brown eyes. Beth and Penny liked fashion very much, but they did not have a lot of money. They bought handbags and shoes in sales and on the Internet. They bought most of their clothes in second-hand shops. Beth was good at sewing. She could alter clothes to fit her and Penny.

At the beginning of winter, Beth wanted a new warm coat. She walked to work every day, and it was often very cold. She found a very good coat in a second-hand shop. It was a coat for a man. It was grey and the material was made from cashmere and wool. But there was a hole in one of the sleeves, so it was very cheap. Beth paid five pounds for the coat. She took it home and cut it up. She made a beautiful warm coat for herself. It was very stylish and it looked very, very expensive. Even at the department store, no one realized that Beth had made her own coat.

"Beth's family must have a lot of money," said the other secretaries. "Her clothes are fabulous."

One night in January, Penny came home from work late. Beth was sitting in the living room watching TV.

"Beth! Beth! I have great news!" Penny shouted as she walked into the living room.

Beth smiled at her friend. "You are very excited. What

happened?"

"The boss called me into her office. They want me to go and work in the head office in London! Isn't it wonderful?"

Beth laughed. "Of course, Mike is in London, so I guess you said 'yes'!"

Mike was Penny's boyfriend. He was working for a computer company in London. He and Penny could not see each other very much. Penny missed him.

"Of course I said 'yes'! Mike and I will be in the same city! I will be able to see him all the time!"

"I'm so happy for you," said Beth. "It's great news. When will you move to London?"

"At the end of the month! I can't wait!" said Penny. Then she looked serious. "There is only one bad thing."

"What's that?" asked Beth.

"I don't want to leave you. I will miss you very much. And this flat is too expensive for one person. What will you do?"

Beth stood up and hugged her friend. "Don't worry. I will think of something," she said. "Maybe I can find a cheap flat for one person."

Two days later Penny called Beth at work. "They are hiring a new person to do my job here. Her name is Margot Rottle. She is moving from Newcastle to Manchester. She asked about a flat. She can take my place in our flat. That's good news, isn't it?"

Beth was not sure. Beth was shy. She didn't know if she wanted to share a flat with a stranger. But she didn't want Penny to worry about her. So Beth agreed. Mike drove up from London at the end of January. Beth, Penny and Mike packed Penny's belongings into the car.

Penny and Beth hugged, and they both cried a little.

"I know you won't be lonely," said Penny. "Margot will move into the flat next week. So you will have a new friend. I will come to Manchester soon to see you, and then I will meet Margot. And you must come to London for a weekend as soon as I find somewhere to live."

Beth smiled. "I'll do that," she said. "Good luck!"

Mike and Penny got into the car and drove away.

Beth went back into the flat building and slowly climbed the stairs. She felt lonely.

The Legacy

I will miss Penny so much, she thought. *I hope Margot is nice.*

2. A COLD WET DAY

It was the end of the first week in February. Beth was walking home from work. It was cold and raining heavily. There was a lot of water on the road. Every time a car went past her, water sprayed up from the road. The bottom of her coat and her boots were very wet.

Beth was uncomfortable. She was also unhappy. Penny sent texts and emails every day. She was enjoying London very much.

Beth missed Penny a lot. The new flatmate, Margot, was so different from Penny. Margot always forgot to buy food. Then she ate the food that Beth had bought. She didn't clean the bathroom. She used Beth's cosmetics. This made Beth angry. Cosmetics were expensive, and Beth saved for a long time to buy them. After a few days, she asked Margot not to use them. She said, "Please use your own cosmetics, Margot."

Margot seemed surprised. "But why? You have the latest colours. I like your makeup more than mine. And I want to borrow your red handbag tomorrow. It will match my jacket very well. Shall I take it from your bedroom now?"

Beth sighed as she walked along the cold wet footpath. Then she said to herself, *Cheer up. It's not so bad. Penny and I had so much fun together. She was the perfect flatmate. Of course a new flatmate will not be as nice as Penny.*

Then she smiled. *I'm lucky Margot is so much bigger than me. She can take my bags and scarves and jewellery and makeup, but my clothes are all too small for her. She can't take those!*

When Beth reached the flat, Margot was in the bath.

The Legacy

I suppose she will use all the hot water again, thought Beth. *Never mind. I can have a shower in the morning.*

Beth hung her coat up on the door of her closet to dry. She looked around the room. *Margot has been in here again,* she thought. *I wonder why she is always looking in my drawers. I guess she is looking for things to borrow. I am pleased I have a password on my computer. Otherwise I guess she would read all my emails too.*

Beth went into the kitchen. She poured herself a glass of wine and started to cook dinner for herself. She was making pasta with tomato and cauliflower sauce when Margot walked in.

"I got wet coming back from work," said Margot. "So I took a bath to warm myself up." Margot took the bottle of wine out of the refrigerator and poured herself a glass.

"What are you cooking?" she asked Beth.

"I'm making myself some pasta for dinner," answered Beth. "I will be finished soon and then you can have the kitchen."

"Oh, I forgot to go shopping today. I'll just have some of your pasta," said Margot.

"I am only cooking enough for one person," said Beth. She felt angry.

Margot looked in the pot. "I think there is enough for two," she said. "You don't eat very much. Call me when it is ready."

Margot went into the living room and turned on the TV.

Beth felt very, very angry, but she finished cooking the pasta and made a salad with salami and peppers. She carried the food into the living room and put it on the small dining table in the corner. She put plates and forks on the table.

"Oh, it's ready," said Margot. "Good. Would you like another glass of wine?"

Margot went into the kitchen and brought out the bottle of wine from the refrigerator.

"There's not very much left," she said. She poured a full glass for herself and poured a little into Beth's glass.

Beth stopped feeling angry. She laughed. "Margot, you are unbelievable! That wine is mine! I bought it! Since you have been in this flat you haven't bought any food or drink! You don't clean, and you don't cook. It is not a good idea for us to share a flat. I think you should find another place to live."

Margot looked surprised. "Why? I pay the rent. You can't live here alone. The rent is too expensive. I thought you were a nice person, but you complain all the time. You are not fun to share with."

I will have to find somewhere else to live, thought Beth. *I can't live with Margot and I don't think she will go away.*

They ate in silence. Then Margot said suddenly, "I forgot. There was a letter for you in mailbox. It came from New Zealand. Who writes letters these days? Everyone uses the Internet."

Margot put her hand in her pocket and took out the letter. She didn't give it to Beth.

"It is from someone called W. V. Whitley-Sneddon. It is written in ink. The back of the envelope got wet in the rain. I can't read the address, but the postmark on the stamp says 'Christchurch, New Zealand'. It must be a relative of yours. Who is it?"

"I don't know!" said Beth. "Would you give me my letter please?"

"OK," Margot gave Beth the letter. Margot stood up and went back to the sofa in front of the TV. She turned the volume up very loud. She lay down on the sofa.

Beth went to her bedroom and sat on the bed. She opened the letter and read it. She was very surprised. Then she read it again.

3. THE LETTER

--- *My dear Great-Niece Beth,*

I think you will be surprised to receive this letter. My name is William Victor Whitley-Sneddon. Your grandfather was my brother. Many years ago, I had a terrible argument with my father, your great-grandfather. I left Scotland and went to America. Later, I moved to New Zealand. I was very angry, and I never communicated with my father or brother again.

I am old now, and I am ill. I think I will die soon. I must communicate with my family before I die. I asked a friend to find my relatives on the Internet. He told me your father, my nephew, died a long time ago. He told me you have a mother living in Leeds, but you are my only blood relative, so I am writing to you.

Please come to New Zealand to visit me. It is very important. I have many things to tell you, and a treasure to give you. It is very valuable. I know you are only 24 years old. I guess you do not have very much money. So I have asked my lawyer to send money for an airplane ticket to a lawyer in Manchester. The name of the law office is Peacock and Adderly. If you go there and show them your passport, they will give you the money.

You will want to show this letter to your mother. That is OK. But please do not talk to anyone else about it. I have many secrets to tell you. The valuable thing I want to give you is a secret too.

Please come as soon as possible. I don't think there is much time.
Your loving great-uncle,
William Victor Whitley-Sneddon

4. WHAT ARE YOU DOING?

Beth put the letter under her pillow and went back to the living room. She picked up the dirty dishes and glasses and took them to the kitchen. Margot was still lying on the sofa. Beth washed the dishes and cleaned the kitchen. She was tired and wanted to go to bed, so she went to the bathroom to take off her makeup and clean her teeth. When she opened her bedroom door, she saw Margot. Margot was reading the letter!

"What are you doing?" Beth shouted. "That's my letter! It's private! Give it to me!" Margot laughed at her. "Don't be so stupid! It's only a letter!" Margot threw the letter on the bed and went out.

Beth changed into her pyjamas and got into bed, but she couldn't sleep.

It is a very strange letter, she thought. *Should I go to New Zealand? I don't know what to do. I will go and see my mother. Maybe she knows something about Great-Uncle William.*

It was after midnight when Beth finally fell asleep.

5. BETH'S MOTHER

The next day was Saturday. Beth sent a text message to her mother. Then she walked to the station and took a train to Leeds. Stephanie, Beth's mother, lived there. She taught French in a local high school.

Stephanie was waiting for Beth at the railway station. They drove to Stephanie's flat in Alwoodley. She had a small flat on the top floor of a big old house.

"I made soup for lunch," said Stephanie. "I will heat it up. Then you can tell me your news while we are eating."

Beth pushed a pile of exam papers and textbooks to one end of the big table in the living room, and sat down. Her mother soon brought big steaming bowls of vegetable soup, bread and cheese to the table.

"How is Penny?" she asked. "Is she enjoying London?"

"Oh, yes. Very much. She loves being near Mike and she loves her new job," answered Beth.

"And how is the new flat mate? Is she nice?"

"No!" said Beth. "She is not nice at all! I don't like her. I think I will have to find a new flat."

"Oh dear," said Stephanie. "What is the problem?"

Beth told her mother all about Margot.

"I agree," said Stephanie. "I don't think she is a good person to live with. But what will you do? It will be expensive to rent a flat by yourself."

"I think I will give up the flat and take a month's vacation. I might go on a trip to New Zealand," said Beth.

"What?" Stephanie was amazed. "Why New Zealand?"

Beth took the letter out of her bag and gave it to her mother.

"Read this," she said.

Stephanie read the letter.

"This is a big surprise," she said.

"Do you know anything about this man, William Victor Whitley-Sneddon?" asked Beth.

"I don't know much about your father's family," said Stephanie. "Your father and I met in France. He was working in a vineyard, and I was staying with a local family and going to a language school. We fell in love, and got married about three months later. We had our wedding at the vineyard. It was wonderful. We lived in a small house in the town. We were married only six months when he was killed in the car accident. You were born eight months later.

"What can I remember? His family came from Scotland. Your father grew up on a farm. I think his grandfather had a very big house somewhere. The grandfather owned the farm. And his son, your grandfather, lived on the farm. Gerald, your father, didn't want to be a farmer. He wanted to learn how to make wine, so he went to France. This letter talks about something very valuable, a treasure, but I don't think your father's family was rich. Your father didn't have any money. We were very poor when we got married, but it didn't matter, we were so much in love."

"Why didn't you go to Scotland and see my father's family when you came back from France?" asked Beth. "It was very difficult for you. You had me. I was very young and you had no money. Maybe they would have helped you."

"I don't know," said Stephanie. "Maybe because your father never talked about his family very much. Or maybe I wanted to do everything for you by myself."

"So what do you think I should do?" asked Beth. "Should I go to New Zealand?"

"I think you should go and see the lawyer in Manchester. If he gives you enough money, I think you should go to New Zealand. It will be an adventure. I don't think this old man in New Zealand will have a great treasure to give you. He wrote 'very valuable' but it might just be some photographs or some letters. But it will be nice for you to meet someone from your father's family. So I think you should go. Have a holiday. Now, how about some coffee? Then maybe we can go for a walk."

6. A VERY BUSY WEEK

At lunchtime on Monday, Beth went to the office of Peacock and Adderly. She had to wait for a few minutes, and then the clerk said, "Mr Adderly will see you now."

The clerk took Beth into the lawyer's office.

"My name is Beth Whitley-Sneddon. I believe some money was sent from New Zealand for me," she said.

"Yes, that's right," said Mr Adderly. "It is a little unusual. I got a letter from a lawyer in Christchurch, New Zealand last week. Then on Friday, the money was paid into our bank account. I will give you a cheque. Do you have your passport?"

Beth showed Mr Adderly her passport. He gave her a cheque for 3,000 pounds.

"Thank you," said Beth.

"Please sign this paper," said Mr Adderly. "It says that you received the money from us."

Beth signed the paper. Then she stood up to leave the office. At the door she stopped. "I have a question," she said. "Do you know anything about my great-uncle? The man who sent the money?"

"No. Nothing," said the lawyer. "I don't know the lawyer in Christchurch either. I guess he found our firm on the Internet."

That night Beth sat on her bed with her laptop computer. She searched for the cost of airfares from Manchester to Christchurch. It seemed that she could buy a return ticket for less than 2000 pounds.

Good, thought Beth. *I have enough money. I can go to New Zealand.*

Beth checked all the airlines. She wanted a very cheap flight, but

The Legacy

the cheapest had so many stops and took so long. She decided the best route was from Manchester to Abu Dhabi; then from Abu Dhabi to Brisbane in Australia, and then from Brisbane to Christchurch.

Beth booked a flight for the next Saturday.

I have four days to get ready! It's not very long, but my Great-Uncle William told me to come as soon as possible!

Beth found an address for W. V. Whitley-Sneddon in Christchurch on the Internet, but she couldn't find a telephone number, so she wrote a letter.

--- 'Dear Great-Uncle William,

I was very surprised to get your letter. I talked to my mother about it. She told me to visit you. I have booked my tickets and I will arrive in Christchurch next Sunday. Thank you for sending the money. I am very excited and I am looking forward to meeting you,

Love Beth'---

I will post it tomorrow, thought Beth. *Maybe I will arrive in Christchurch before the letter is delivered, but maybe not.*

The next day Beth said to her boss, "I am very sorry, but I have to go to New Zealand. I will be away for about one month. My great-uncle is very ill. Maybe he will die soon. I am his only relative. So I must go."

"Of course you must go," said her boss. "I will miss you. You are the best secretary I have ever had. So please don't stay away too long."

Beth was very busy. She told Margot she was giving up the flat and going away.

"I will pay half the rent for one month," said Beth. "So you have one month to find a new flatmate."

Margot was angry. "You're lucky. You can just go away. Where are you going? What am I going to do?"

Beth didn't answer.

Margot looked everywhere in the flat. She wanted to know where Beth was going.

Beth finished work on Thursday. As soon as she got back to the flat, she sent a text to Penny.

---'*Manchester is so grey and boring without you. I am taking a holiday to New Zealand. I will send you lots of emails and photographs from there*'.---

Penny was very surprised. She called Beth to talk about it. Beth and Penny talked on the telephone for a long time. Margot stood outside the door and listened.

When Beth finished talking to Penny, Margot came into her bedroom.

"You are going to New Zealand, aren't you?" she said.

"Yes, I am," answered Beth.

"It's not fair," said Margot. "You have everything. You have beautiful, expensive clothes. You have a rich family. You can travel. I don't have anything."

Shall I tell her my clothes come from sales and second-hand shops? thought Beth. *Shall I tell her that the trip to New Zealand is a present? Shall I tell her that my family has no money? No. I won't. Why should I? I am leaving this flat, and I am never coming back here. If I am lucky, I will never see Margot again.*

"I'm busy, Margot," said Beth. "I have to pack all my clothes and belongings. And I'm tired. Please go away."

Margot went out of the room and shut the door very loudly.

On Friday, Margot didn't go to work. She called the insurance company, and told them she was ill.

Beth was angry. *I thought I would have the flat to myself. Why is she staying home today? I am sure she is not ill. What does she want?*

The moving company came to the door. Beth asked them to come inside to carry her boxes out to the truck. She planned to send most of her clothes and belongings to her mother in Leeds.

While Beth was talking to the moving men, Margot went into the living room and found Beth's handbag. She took out Beth's air tickets and read them. Margot liked knowing everything.

The next morning, Beth left the flat. She had her suitcase, her backpack and her handbag. She left the flat keys on the table, and took a taxi to the airport. Margot didn't get up until Beth had left the flat. She looked in the refrigerator. There was almost no food. She looked in Beth's bedroom and in the bathroom. Beth's clothes and accessories and cosmetics were all gone. Margot felt angry.

Margot thought about the letter. She remembered that Beth's great-uncle was going to give her a treasure.

They are rich people, she thought. *Beth has everything. It's not fair. I don't have anything. I wonder what the treasure is.*

She remembered the name of Beth's great-uncle. So she made herself a cup of tea and took out her laptop computer. She searched for the name 'William Victor Whitley-Sneddon'. Margot was surprised. It seemed that he was a specialist in old Italian art. It seemed that he was famous. He had worked in the USA. Then he had gone to New Zealand and worked in a university there. He was retired now.

University professors don't earn much money, but maybe he found a treasure when he was working, thought Margot. *I guess it's some old writing or painting. Beth is welcome to it. It's not like jewels or gold or money!*

7. SILAS

Margot had a brother called Silas. He was living in Australia. Silas was not a nice person. When he lived in England, he was always in trouble. He got into fights and he stole things. He killed a man in a fight outside a pub. In the beginning, the police didn't know who did it, but Silas thought they would soon find out. So he stole money from his grandmother and bought an air ticket to Australia. In Australia he joined a gang. The gang made money from drugs and gambling. Some members also stole expensive cars, changed the license plates, and sold them. It was a very large and well-organised gang. Silas was part of the group that stole cars. The gang members made a lot of money, but most of the money went to the leader of the gang. He was called Rocco. The normal gang members never met Rocco. He lived in a big and beautiful house in an expensive part of the city. His neighbours thought he was a successful businessman.

Silas thought he was smarter than Rocco and the others.

These Australians are very stupid, he thought. *The leader of the car thieves finds a car for me to steal in Brisbane. I steal it, and then later, another member of the gang sells it for a hundred thousand dollars in Melbourne. I only get ten thousand dollars and the guy in Melbourne gets the same. The rest of the money goes to Rocco. I can make more money than that.*

Silas continued to work with the gang, but he sometimes worked alone. He stole cars and sold them to the gang's clients. He sold them for a much lower price but he still made a lot of money. He kept all the money and spent it. But, of course, Rocco found out.

On the Thursday before Beth left to go to New Zealand, two gang members, Spike and Boots, came to Silas' flat. They put him in the back of a van and drove him to Rocco's office in the centre of the city. Silas was very frightened.

Rocco told Silas that he must pay back all the money from the car sales.

"I want a hundred and twenty thousand dollars by next Friday," said Rocco. "If I don't get the money, I will kill you."

"But I don't have the money…."

Just then, the phone rang. Rocco picked up the phone.

"Yes? Yes, dear. No. I haven't forgotten. Don't worry, I'll find something very, very special. Yes. I'll be home for dinner."

Rocco hung up the telephone and sighed. "My wife has joined an art and history society. It's her latest craze. The society meets in members' houses once a month. In two weeks they will come to our house. My wife wants something very special to show them. Something unique. Where am I going to find something like that? I am a busy man. Even if I can find something very old and special, it will probably cost me a lot of money."

He looked at Silas. "And you have stolen a lot of money. The money you got for those cars was mine! And I want it back. Next Friday, or you're dead!"

Spike and Boots took Silas back out onto the street and pushed him into the van. "He's not serious, is he?" asked Silas. "He won't kill me."

Spike looked at him. "Of course he's serious. Find the money and give it to him, or you're dead."

Boots laughed. "Don't think you can run away. One of us will be watching you day and night. You can't escape. So find the money!"

They drove Silas back to his flat. *What can I do?* Silas asked himself. *I have to get away. I spent all the money, I only have about five thousand dollars and they say they will kill me!*

Boots came into the flat with Silas. He sat down and turned on the television. "Do you have any beer?" he asked.

Silas gave Boots a can of beer. Then he went into his bedroom.

"What are you doing?" shouted Boots. "Don't get any crazy ideas about climbing out the window. Even if you get away from me, Rocco will find you."

"I'm going to work on my computer," said Silas. "I have to work out how to get the money."

Silas sat on the bed and put his head in his hands. I am really in trouble. I need help! Maybe Margot can help me. She said she had moved into a flat with a rich girl. Maybe she can find the money for me.

8. MARGOT HAS AN IDEA

Silas emailed Margot.

---*'I am in terrible trouble. I need money. A lot of money.'*---

He was lucky. She was on her computer, so she answered quickly.

--- *'What have you done now? I don't have any money. I thought you had a good scheme and were making a lot of money.'*---

Silas went to the door of his bedroom and looked at Boots. Boots was drinking another can of beer. He was watching a sports programme on the TV. He had the volume up very loud. Silas quietly closed the door to his bedroom and sent another email.

---*'Can we talk on Skype?'*--- he wrote.

Soon he was talking to Margot on Skype. He told her all about his problems.

"The guy is crazy," he said. "He's talking about killing me. And then the next minute he's talking about how his wife wants some unique and amazing work of art to show her friends in the art and history society."

Margot was worried.

"You are an idiot, Silas!"

Margot was a very selfish person, but she didn't want Rocco to murder her brother. Then, she had an idea.

"My flatmate is on her way to New Zealand. Her great-uncle is going to give her a treasure. She's a very shy and gentle person. It would be easy to steal the treasure from her."

"Margot!" said Silas. "What is the treasure? Could I sell it for a hundred and twenty thousand dollars?"

"I don't know what it is," said Margot. "Beth didn't know either."
"It's probably something really stupid, like a family photograph!"
Silas didn't think Margot was helping him at all.
"No, no! Silas," said Margot. "Let me explain."
"This old guy, Beth's great-uncle, is a specialist in old Italian art. He's very famous. He says the treasure is very valuable. I guess that it is some old Italian picture or writing or something like that. It seems that it is also a secret, so he will probably keep it in his house.
"Rocco's wife wants something unique and special to show her friends in the art and history society. So do a deal with Rocco. Tell him you can get him something really unique and valuable. Tell him it's hidden in an old man's house in Christchurch, New Zealand. Tell him you will give it to him instead of the hundred and twenty thousand dollars. Even if it doesn't work, it will give you more time to find the money or to escape."
Silas thought about it. He didn't think it was a very good idea, but he didn't have a better idea.
"OK," he said. "I'll try it. If Rocco agrees, I'll go to New Zealand and try to steal this treasure. How will I find this woman, Beth?"
"That's easy," said Margot. "Her name's Beth Whitley-Sneddon. She will be stopping in Brisbane on the way to New Zealand. I'll give you the flight number. Travel on the same flight as her from Brisbane to Christchurch. You will recognize her. She's tall, thin and wears designer clothes."
"How would I know what designer clothes look like?" asked Silas.
Margot sighed. "You are an idiot. Walk around the departure lounge before the plane leaves Brisbane. Her backpack is made from red leather. You'll find her. Even if you miss her, you can find her uncle. His name's William Victor Whitley-Sneddon."
"OK," he said. "I'll talk to Rocco. I hope he agrees. Otherwise I will be a dead man."

9. BRISBANE AIRPORT

Beth enjoyed the flight from Manchester to Abu Dhabi very much, but the flight from Abu Dhabi to Brisbane was very long. She felt excited and worried at the same time. She couldn't sleep. When she got off the plane in Brisbane, she didn't feel good.

I have three hours to wait here, she thought. *Then it's another three and a half hours to Christchurch. I think I should walk around the airport. Maybe I will start to feel better.*

Beth walked around the shops in the airport. She saw a duty-free shop.

I didn't buy anything for Great-Uncle William. I should take him a present. I wonder what he would like.

Beth looked in the duty-free shop. She decided to buy her great-uncle a bottle of Scotch whisky. She went to the sales counter.

"May I see your boarding pass?" asked the salesman.

Beth took out her boarding pass and put it on the counter in front of the man.

"That's OK," he said. Beth paid for the whisky and walked to the departure gate for the flight to Christchurch. She bought a bottle of water from a vending machine and sat down to wait. A man in a leather jacket was walking around the departure lounge. He seemed to be looking for someone.

Suddenly she heard her name. There was an announcement.

"Would Ms Whitley-Sneddon, passenger for Christchurch, please go immediately to the Information Desk near Gate 81."

Beth jumped up. *I wonder what's wrong.*

She hurried to the Information Desk. She didn't notice that the man in a leather jacket followed her.

Beth found the Information Desk easily. She went up to the woman behind the desk. The man in the leather jacket came up and stood very close behind her.

A tall brown-haired man was standing next to the counter. Beth thought he wanted to talk to a member of staff. She stopped and waited. He smiled at her.

"Go ahead," he said.

"I am Beth Whitley-Sneddon," she said to the woman behind the desk. "I heard my name on the announcement."

"Oh, yes," said the woman. "Do you have some ID?"

Beth showed the woman her passport.

"You left your boarding pass in the duty-free shop," said the woman.

"Oh, no!" said Beth. "How could I be so stupid?"

The woman laughed. "People do it all the time. Don't worry!"

She gave the boarding pass to Beth.

"Thank you," said Beth. She turned to go back to the departure gate.

The tall brown-haired man next to the counter spoke to Beth.

"Excuse me, but …"

Beth didn't hear him. She walked off quickly, holding her boarding pass.

"Can I help you?" said the woman to the man in the leather jacket.

"No, thanks," he answered. He walked away.

Beth went back to the departure lounge.

I still have to wait two hours, she thought. She had an idea. *I will see if I can find out some information about my father's family. I wanted to do it before I left Manchester, but I was so busy.*

Beth took her iPad out of her bag and started searching. It was very difficult. She had the name, 'Whitley-Sneddon', and she knew the year her father was born. Her mother said the family had a big house and a farm in Scotland. Finally, she found some old newspaper reports.

So I know my father's name was Gerald. It seems that a man called Alan Whitley-Sneddon was chairman of a sheep farmers association in nineteen eighty one. He lived near Dumfries in Scotland. That might be my grandfather. And here is another newspaper report about a man called George Whitley-Sneddon. It is the notice of his death. He died in nineteen ninety, aged eighty-five. His home was called Kirk House and it was near Dumfries too. I wonder if I can find a death notice for Alan Whitley-Sneddon.

She typed in --- *'Obituary Alan Whitley-Sneddon'*---, and pressed return.

Here it is!

--- *'Alan Whitley-Sneddon*

Published Wednesday 20 August 2012

Whitley-Sneddon, Alan. Died peacefully after a long illness, at Dumfries Hospital, on 17th August, 2013, aged 82 years. His home was Hill Top Farm, Lochmaben. (Chairman of the Dumfries and Galloway Sheep Farmers Association for twenty years). Beloved husband of the late Isobel, father of the late Gerald, and brother of William (believed to be residing in America).'---

Beth heard the boarding announcement for her flight, so she turned her iPad off and joined the line of people waiting to board the plane.

I think I found the right family, she thought. *So now I know a little more. When I get a chance, I will try to find a death notice for my father.*

10. FLIGHT TO CHRISTCHURCH

Beth had a seat next to the window.
Only three and a half hours left, she thought. *I am so tired. I'll try to sleep.*
More than three hours later, Beth woke up suddenly.
A flight attendant was talking to her.
"We will be landing soon," he said. "Could you fasten your seat belt please?"
"Oh, sure," answered Beth.
She fastened her seat belt. Beth looked out of the plane window. They were flying lower and lower. She could see high mountains. It was the end of summer in New Zealand, but the tops of the mountains were white with snow and ice. Away from the mountains, the land was very flat.
The man sitting next to Beth was looking out of the window too.
"Is this your first time to visit Christchurch?" he asked Beth.
"It's my first time to visit New Zealand," answered Beth.
"You're from England, aren't you?" said the man.
"That's right," said Beth.
Soon Beth could see a very wide river. The water was a greenish-blue.
"That's the Waimakariri River," said the man.
"The land is so flat," said Beth.
"Yes," said the man. "On this side of the mountains, the land is very flat. The weather is often very hot and dry. We had only a little rain this summer. It was very bad for farming. But on the east side of the mountains, it is like another world. There are many hills. It rains a

lot and everything is very green."

"Are you a farmer?" asked Beth.

The man laughed. "Yes, I am a farmer. I have a sheep farm at the bottom of those mountains."

11. ARRIVING IN CHRISTCHURCH

After the plane landed, Beth went through customs and immigration and collected her suitcase. The local time was 3:30pm.

Now, what shall I do? Shall I find a hotel? No, I think I will go to Great-Uncle William's house. I will meet him. Maybe I can stay with him. If I can't, I will find a hotel nearby.

She walked out of the airport. It was windy, and the air was very hot and dry. She saw a row of taxis and walked towards them. The man from the plane was walking towards the car park.

"Are you OK?" he asked.

"Yes, thank you. I'm going to take a taxi to my uncle's house."

"Good. What do you think of this wind? We call it the Norwester."

"I hope it doesn't last long," said Beth.

"It probably won't. Enjoy your time in New Zealand," said the man and he walked away.

She got into the first taxi in the line and gave the driver the address.

"Fendalton," he said. "We will be there in ten minutes."

Silas was watching from the entrance to the terminal. When he saw Beth get into a taxi, he ran to the next taxi in the line.

"Follow that taxi," he said, pointing to Beth's taxi.

"Are you crazy?" said the driver. "Do you think this is a TV show? I don't follow other taxis. Give me an address or get out of my car."

As Silas got out of the taxi, he saw Beth's taxi disappearing in the distance.

Now what will I do? thought Silas. *I will have to find out where the old man lives.*

Beth's taxi pulled up in a wide, quiet street. Great-Uncle William's house was not large, but the garden was very big and beautiful.

Beth paid the driver and got out of the taxi. The driver took her bag out of the boot, got back in the taxi, and drove away.

Beth opened the white wooden gate and walked down the garden path towards the front door. It was very quiet. She rang the doorbell and knocked on the door. No one came.

Maybe Great-Uncle William is out, thought Beth. *Or maybe he is deaf. Many old people can't hear well. I'll go around to the back of the house, and try again.*

She walked around to the back of the house. She tried knocking on the door and shouting.

"Do you want something?"

It was a woman's voice. Beth was surprised. She turned around. There was a woman standing at the fence between Great-Uncle William's house and the house next door.

"Uh, yes. I have come to visit Mr Whitley-Sneddon. Is he out?"

The woman looked closely at Beth.

"You have a suitcase and a duty-free bag," she said. "Did you come to stay?"

"Yes. William Whitley-Sneddon is my great-uncle. He invited me here."

The woman said, "Come here to my house. I will make you a cup of tea. You look very tired."

Beth wheeled her suitcase down the path and through the gate. She went into the garden of the house next door. The woman was waiting for her. She was about sixty years old. She had short white hair and very bright blue eyes.

"It's lucky I heard you," she said. "I was bringing in the laundry. My name is Clara, Clara Bolton. Come into the house, and I will make you a cup of tea."

Beth followed Clara down the hallway and into a big kitchen at the back of the house. Beth sat down at the kitchen table. Clara made tea and put two cups on the table. She sat down opposite Beth.

"You said you are Mr Whitley-Sneddon's niece," said Clara.

"Great-niece," explained Beth. "He wrote to me and invited me to visit him. Is he out? Do you think he will come back soon?"

Clara put down her tea cup, and put her hand on top of Beth's.

"My dear. I am very sorry to tell you this. But Mr Whitley-Sneddon died five days ago."

Beth felt dizzy. "Oh, no! He wrote in his letter that he was sick. He wrote that he would die soon, but I didn't think he would die so quickly! What happened? Did you know him well?"

"No, I didn't know him well. He came here when he retired from the university. He was a professor there. So I guess I should call him Professor Whitley-Sneddon or Dr Whitley-Sneddon. He was a nice man. He worked in his garden, and I think he read and wrote a lot. I saw him on the street one day, and he told me he was going to work in the university library. He always said 'good morning' or 'good afternoon', and we talked about the garden or the weather. That was all."

"So how did he die?" asked Beth.

"I don't know. During the summer I didn't see him in the garden very much. He used to walk everywhere, but since Christmas he often used taxis. It was the summer holidays and I was very busy. My grandchildren came to stay. Then about two weeks ago, he came to my door. He looked very ill. He asked me to post some letters. One of the letters was addressed to Miss B Whitley-Sneddon. Is that you?"

"Yes. That's why I came. He asked me to. I had never met him. He was my father's uncle. My father died before I was born, and I never met his family."

"Two days later, an ambulance came. Then your great-uncle died a week later in hospital," Clara told Beth.

Beth thought about her great-uncle. She felt very sad.

He must have been lonely. And I guess he never knew that I was coming.

"Did he have any friends?" Beth asked Clara.

"When he first came here, he sometimes had visitors. They all looked old to me. Maybe they have died now. In the past year, there has only been one. A young man came to visit him. Since Christmas he came often. He brought groceries and I saw him cleaning sometimes. Maybe he was an ex-student. I saw him at the funeral."

"It was nice of you to go to the funeral," said Beth.

"He was my neighbour, so of course I went. There were not many people there. There were only some people from the university, the young man who used to come here, and a lawyer. The young man didn't speak to me, but the lawyer did. He was your great-uncle's lawyer. He told me the only family was in England. He said that he was going to write to them."

Clara gave Beth another cup of tea. "You have had a shock, and I can see you are very tired. Where are you going to stay?" she asked. "You can stay here, if you like."

"Oh, no. No. It's OK. I will find a hotel. I will find one on the Internet."

"Just a minute," said Clara. "I'm going to make a phone call."

Clara went out of the kitchen. When she came back, she had some keys in her hand.

"When I met the lawyer at the funeral, he gave me his business card. And he gave me a set of keys to your great-uncle's house. 'In case of emergencies', he said. I called him. He says you can stay in the house if you want. Do you want to do that?"

Beth was tired and confused. She couldn't think properly.

"Yes. OK. Yes. I will stay in the house."

Clara put some milk and tea bags in a basket. "After the funeral, I went into the house and emptied the refrigerator," she told Beth. "I tidied up the house a little. But everything was very clean and neat. I am sure you will be comfortable."

They went back to her great-uncle's house. Clara turned on the electricity supply.

"It will take an hour or more for the hot water to heat up," she said.

She put the milk in the refrigerator. She found sheets and pillowcases and made up a bed for Beth in a little bedroom at the back of the house. Then she gave the house keys to Beth, said 'goodbye' and left.

Beth found a nightdress in her suitcase. She got into bed and fell asleep immediately. She slept for twenty hours.

12. GREAT-UNCLE WILLIAM'S HOUSE

When Beth finally woke up, she was very confused. She looked around the room. It was small and looked very old fashioned. It looked like no one used it.

I don't know this room, she thought. *Where am I?*

Then she saw her suitcase and backpack. She remembered everything.

She got out of bed and went to the kitchen. There was a basket on the table. On top of the basket was a note from Clara.

--- *'I came in but you were sleeping. Your great-uncle's lawyer called. He wants to talk to you. He asked if you would please contact him. There is no telephone in the house. If you want to call the lawyer, please come over.'* ---

Beth looked in the basket. Clara had made muffins. She had put a little jar of jam and a pot of butter in the basket too.

Beth realized she was very thirsty and very hungry. She made a cup of tea and ate the muffins. Then she went back to the bedroom and found a sundress and a pair of sandals. The bathroom was next to her bedroom. She took a shower, washed her hair and dressed.

I'll look around the house, she thought. *So far, I have only seen the kitchen, that little bedroom and the bathroom.*

The first room she went into was Great-Uncle William's bedroom. It was on the other side of the bathroom. It was very tidy. The furniture was old, but well-polished. There was a bed, a set of drawers, an armchair and a small table. The table was next to the bed. It had a clock and packets of medicine on it. There was a painting on the wall. She walked over and looked at the painting. It was a picture of a stone house. It looked like a house in Scotland.

Beth felt strange.

I don't like being in this room, she thought. *It is Great-Uncle William's room. Maybe he wouldn't like me to be in here.*

She went out quickly and walked along the hallway towards the front door. There was a door to the left and a door to the right.

I'll go to the left first, she thought.

Beth walked into a living room. It was a lovely room. The sun was coming in through the big windows at the front and side of the room. The furniture was old, but looked very comfortable. The walls were covered with paintings and there was a big Persian carpet on the floor.

I'll come back and sit in this room later, Beth thought. *It is a nice room to relax in.*

She went back to the hallway and tried the door to the right.

This room was an office. Two walls had bookshelves from floor to ceiling. The desk in the middle of the room was covered in piles of paper. There was a computer, printer and scanner on a table under the side window. Another table was covered in rolls of paper. Under the big window at the front of the room was a row of metal cabinets.

When Beth saw the computer, she thought, *I should send an email to my mother.*

She went back to the small bedroom and took out her iPad.

I wonder if I can access the Internet on my iPad from here.

She tried, but she could not.

I guess Great-Uncle William didn't have WI-FI. I wonder if his computer is connected to the Internet.

She went back to the office and turned on the computer, but she could not use it. It was password protected.

I wonder why Great-Uncle William was worried about people using his computer. He didn't share his office or his computer with anyone. Sometimes people write their passwords down. Maybe there is a notebook or something....

Beth tried to open the drawers in the desk. They were all locked. She went to the metal cabinets. They were locked too.

Beth gave up.

Maybe Clara has WI-FI, she thought. *Or maybe I can use her computer.*

She went back to the bedroom, picked up her handbag and went to the kitchen. She saw the house keys sitting on the counter.

I forgot to lock the door last night, she thought. *I am only going next door.*

So I am sure I don't have to lock the door now.

She put the keys in her handbag and walked down the path to the road.

Clara had WI-FI, so Beth could send an email to her mother. She told her mother the trip had been fine, but it was very long. She told her mother that Great-Uncle William had died.

--- *'It was a shock, but I am OK. There is a very nice neighbour. Her name is Clara. She is helping me a lot. I will go to see Great-Uncle William's lawyer. Maybe, after I see him, I will know more.'*---

Beth called the lawyer. They planned to meet at 4:00pm.

"You can take a bus from Fendalton into the city," said the lawyer. "Or a taxi."

Beth looked at her watch. It was 2:30pm.

"What time should I leave here to get to the city?" she asked Clara.

"Oh, there is a bus from the school. It will take about fifteen minutes. The lawyer's office is in Cashel Street, isn't it? So if you get off the bus at Montreal Street, it will only be a five-minute walk. Why don't you catch the three-fifteen bus? We'll have a cup of coffee before you go."

Thank you," said Beth.

"And you might be lonely, tonight. So please come and have dinner with me."

"I'd like that," said Beth. "You are very kind."

13. SILAS IN NEW ZEALAND

When Silas told Rocco about the treasure, Rocco asked his secretary to check up on William Whitley-Sneddon. It was true that he was very famous. It also seemed that he had left a very good job in the United States and gone to New Zealand. Rocco thought there was a chance he could get something very good for his wife. And he wouldn't have to pay for it. Of course he still planned to get the $120,000 from Silas, but Silas didn't know that.

I've got nothing to lose, thought Rocco. *I'll let Silas go to New Zealand. I have many friends in Christchurch. They will watch him for me. He won't escape.*

Silas was disappointed when he couldn't follow Beth from the airport, so he went to a bar in the centre of the city and drank a lot of beer. Then he went out into the streets. It was his first time in Christchurch. He had the address of a cheap hotel, but he got lost. He wandered into a large park. He felt very tired, so he lay down on a park bench and fell asleep.

In the morning he was woken up by joggers and cyclists in the park. He found an Internet café and ate breakfast. Then he searched for W. Whitley-Sneddon on the Internet and found an address. He sent an email to Margot, telling her he was now in Christchurch. He also sent an email to Rocco saying that he was working on how to steal the treasure. Then he walked to the hotel and checked in. He took a shower and felt tired again, so he lay down on the bed, and went to sleep. It was lunchtime when he woke up.

No hurry, he thought. *If the treasure is in the old man's house, night will be a better time to break in. But I'll go and have a look at the house. I'll take a bus.*

I am sure it will be easy to find.

While Beth and Clara were drinking coffee, Silas walked up to the gate of Great-Uncle William's house, and checked the street number.

He looked around. The street was empty. He walked down the path, and around to the back of the house. He looked in the windows. He couldn't see anyone inside. He knocked on the back door. No one came to the door. He turned the door handle. The door opened!

This is easy, thought Silas. *No one is home. So I will go in and see if I can find anything valuable. I will steal the treasure for Rocco, but maybe I can steal something for myself as well.*

He went into the house and shut the door. He looked in all the rooms. He saw Beth's suitcase and backpack on the floor of one of the rooms.

I'm sure I could sell that backpack and that suitcase for some money, he thought

He looked at the computer in the office. *I could steal that. But it is big, and old and heavy. I need a car or van to take big things away.*

He tried to open the drawers in the desk and the cabinets. He looked in the cabinets in the living room and in the closets in the bedrooms. He didn't find anything.

I could break open those drawers and cabinets in the office, but maybe I won't find anything very valuable. I might find some things to steal but if I take them, they will become worried about burglars. They will lock the house carefully. Maybe they will tell the police. I should wait until I can find out what Beth's great-uncle is going to give her.

At 3:00 pm, Beth came back to the house. Silas heard someone walking down the path and up to the back door. He hid under the bed in Beth's bedroom, but Beth didn't come into the house. She locked the door and went away.

Now I will have to climb out a window, thought Silas.

14. THE LAWYER

Beth enjoyed the bus ride into the centre of the city. The bus drove along a wide street with trees along both sides. Then Beth could see a very large park. Everywhere there were people riding bicycles.

I guess it is popular here, she thought. *They have special road lanes just for bicycles, and it is so flat. It would be easy to ride a bike wherever you wanted to go.*

Beth found the lawyer's office easily. It was in a multi-storied building above a bank.

The lawyer's name was Ivan Pringle. His secretary showed Beth into a corner office. Mr Pringle stood up when Beth came in.

"Ms Whitley-Sneddon," he said. "Thank you for coming. I am very sorry for your loss. I am Ivan Pringle." They shook hands.

"Thank you for seeing me," said Beth.

"Please sit down," said Mr Pringle.

Beth sat down in a comfortable chair opposite Mr Pringle.

"Clara Bolton told me you arrived yesterday. She said you didn't know your uncle had died. It must have been a shock. I'm sorry."

"Yes. It was a shock," said Beth. "I knew he was ill but I didn't know it was so serious. Can you tell me about him?"

Mr Pringle smiled at Beth. "I'm sorry. I don't know very much. I am sure that you have more information than me."

"But I don't know anything!" said Beth. "I never met my great-uncle. I don't know anything about him. He wrote me a letter and asked me to come. He sent some money to pay for the air ticket. You sent the money to the lawyer in Manchester. So you must know all about it!"

"I'm sorry Ms Whitley-Sneddon, but I know very little. Your great-uncle used this law office when he bought his house in Fendalton fifteen years ago. We never saw him again until January this year, when he came in to make a will. Then he came about two weeks ago. He asked me to arrange to send money to Manchester. I believe that money was for you."

"Yes, that's right," said Beth. "But didn't he tell you why he was sending the money? Didn't he tell you why he wanted me to come?"

"No. He didn't say it was for an airfare. He said he wanted me to arrange the money, so I did. I found a lawyer in Manchester and I sent the money. Usually when people send money to relatives, they send it to a bank account. I told him that, but he said he didn't know anything about your bank account. He seemed very tired and sick and worried. So I did what he asked."

"Thank you," said Beth. "I understand. But it is all so strange. I came a long way and my uncle was already dead."

"Yes, I'm very sorry about that. But I want to talk to you about your great-uncle's will."

"His will?" Beth was surprised.

"In his will he left almost everything to you. He left some pictures to a colleague, but everything else is yours. That means his house in Fendalton, the contents of the house, and any money he had in the bank. I will arrange everything. Of course you can stay in the house. It is your house now. If you want to sell it, I will help you.

"When I heard Professor Whitley-Sneddon had died, I went to the hospital and got his keys. I went to the house and took away all the business papers. The Professor was very organized. Everything was together in one folder on his desk. If you need some money, I can give you some. I don't know yet how much money your great-uncle had. We are still doing all the paperwork, but I will call Mrs Bolton and leave a message for you, or I will write you a letter. I hope you plan to stay in Christchurch for at least a few days. It will be much easier."

"Oh," said Beth. "Thank you very much."

"Please call me if you have any questions." Mr Pringle stood up.

Beth stood up too. She walked to the door. She stopped and turned to Mr Pringle.

"Why me?" she asked.

"You were his only blood relative. There wasn't anyone else," answered Mr Pringle.

15. TIM GASKELL

Beth felt very strange when she walked out of the lawyer's office.

Too much has happened, she thought. *Six weeks ago, I was sharing a flat with Penny. We had very little money, but we had a lot of fun. Then Penny went to London, I had a horrible flatmate called Margot, I found out I had a great-uncle called William, he gave me money to come to New Zealand. I came here and now he's dead, and I own a house!*

It was only late afternoon so Beth decided to walk back to Fendalton. She went to a café and ordered a takeout coffee. She took out her iPad and checked the route. It was easy.

I can walk through Hagley Park. That will be nice.

She walked to Hagley Park. It was full of people. There were joggers and cyclists. There were children and family groups. In the distance she could see a group of young people playing cricket. She sat down on a park bench to drink her coffee.

Mr Pringle didn't say anything about secrets, she thought. *He didn't say anything about very valuable things either. Maybe I will never know what Great-Uncle William wanted to tell me. Maybe I will never find the things he wanted to give me.*

Beth finished her coffee and started walking again. As she walked down Fendalton Road, she passed a large supermarket. She went in and bought a bottle of wine, flowers and chocolates for Clara.

Clara has been very kind to me, she thought. *Even if Great-Uncle William had only a little money, I am sure I can afford to spend some to buy gifts for Clara.*

When she arrived at Clara's house, she walked around to the back door and knocked.

"Come in!" shouted Clara. "I have a surprise for you."

Beth walked into the kitchen. Clara was standing by the counter making salad. Beth gave her the gifts.

"Thank you!" said Clara. She hugged Beth. "These are a lovely surprise. It was very sweet of you. And I have a surprise for you! I met him today at the bank!"

There was a young man sitting at the table.

"This is your great-uncle's friend! The one who came here often," explained Clara. "I saw him at the bank and I recognized him. So I went up and introduced myself. I am sure he can tell you a lot."

Beth stared at the young man. "I don't know where, but I've seen you before!"

The young man looked embarrassed. "I'm Tim Gaskell. Yes. You did see me before. In Brisbane Airport."

Clara brought wine glasses and the bottle of wine to the table.

"Why don't you have a nice talk while I finish cooking dinner?"

Tim handed Beth a glass of wine.

"I have to explain," he said. "The day after Professor Whitley-Sneddon's funeral, I had a meeting in Brisbane. Then I had another meeting in Auckland. I was waiting at Brisbane Airport for my flight to Auckland when I heard your name, 'Ms Whitley-Sneddon. Passenger to Christchurch'. It's a very unusual name. I thought it must be you. Beth Whitley-Sneddon. The announcement said to go to the information counter. So I went there too. I wanted to see you. I wanted to talk to you."

"Why?" Beth thought it was very strange.

"Uh. I thought you might be coming to visit the Professor. I thought maybe you didn't know he was dead. I wanted to tell you."

"Why didn't you tell me?" asked Beth.

"I tried to talk to you. But you walked away very quickly. I didn't follow you because I felt stupid. I thought maybe you were not Beth. I thought I would look like an idiot."

Clara came to the table. "I asked Tim to eat dinner with us. I thought it would be nice for you." Clara put down lasagne and salad. "Help yourselves."

Beth told Clara about the bus ride and her walk through the park. "The city is very beautiful. I enjoyed myself."

"What do you think you will do now?" asked Clara. "Will you stay in Christchurch for a while?"

"I think so," said Beth. "I have a job in Manchester, but I think I can stay here for two or three weeks. My uncle left his house to me. I have to have meetings with the lawyer and sign papers. I think I will get a bicycle. A bicycle is perfect for getting around Christchurch."

"My sister is away in Vietnam," said Tim. "Her bicycle is at my flat. You can borrow it."

"Can I?" said Beth. "Are you sure it will be OK?"

"Yes, of course," said Tim. "I will come tomorrow. I will take you to my flat, and you can take the bicycle away."

"Thank you. That will be great."

"Tell Beth about her great-uncle," said Clara. "She came all the way from England and then she never got to meet him. She knows nothing about him."

"That's true," said Beth. "Two weeks ago, I didn't even know I had a great-uncle."

Tim was silent for a few moments. Then he said, "He was an expert in art history. When he was a young man, he studied in England and the United States. He became quite famous. He had a very good job at an important museum in Chicago. But he gave it up and came to Christchurch. He got a job at the university here. After he retired, he stayed in contact with the university. He often came to the university to use the library. I met him when I was a student. He was very kind to me. He knew many people in universities and museums in Europe. He helped me to get a scholarship to study in Italy. I stayed in Italy for five years. Then I spent a year in Germany.

"When I came back to New Zealand I often went to see him. He knew so much, and he was very smart. He helped me with my work. I liked him very much and I was very sorry when he died."

"But you helped him too," said Clara gently. "I saw you cleaning his house and shopping for him."

"I was happy to do it," said Tim. "He was a very nice man. He was my friend."

"What is your work?" asked Beth.

"When I came back here, I got a job at the museum in Christchurch. For many years people gave old paintings to the museum. Often they were very dirty and damaged. No one knew what they were. No one knew what to do with them. So they were stored in the basement. My job is to clean those old paintings and to find out who painted them. Most of the paintings are just old. But sometimes, I find something that is very interesting, or very valuable. Professor Whitley-Sneddon helped me a lot."

Clara took the plates away from the table. She came back with a plate of fruit.

"How did you know I was coming to New Zealand?" asked Beth. "Did my uncle tell you?"

"No," said Tim. "I don't know if he knew you were coming. After Christmas, he became ill. He also became worried about something. I don't know what it was. He asked me to help him find his family in Scotland. I found out that his brother died last year. I found out that his nephew was killed in a car accident more than twenty years ago."

"That was my father," said Beth.

"It took me a long time searching, but then I found that the nephew married in France and there was one child. A daughter. I found your address and gave it to the Professor. He didn't tell me his plan. But I guessed he wanted to contact you. So when I heard the name at Brisbane Airport. I was sure it was you."

"I understand," said Beth. She felt sleepy. "I'm sorry. I slept a long time last night but it has been a strange day, and I feel so tired. I think I should go next door and go to bed."

"Of course!" said Clara. "It takes a long time to adjust between the time zones. It's thirteen hours difference, isn't it?"

Beth thanked Clara for the wonderful meal. Tim said he would come the next day at about 11:00am.

Tim and Clara stood at the door and watched Beth walk down the driveway.

"It's been very hard for her," said Clara. "She is a nice young woman."

"Yes, she is," said Tim. *And she is very, very pretty,* he thought.

16. WHO'S BEEN HERE?

Beth unlocked the back door and went into the house. She turned on the lights, and walked to her bedroom. Suddenly she stopped. The window in her room was open.

It was closed when I went out! What's happened? Is there someone in the house?

Beth ran through all the rooms. She looked in closets and under the beds. There was no one there. In every room she thought that things looked a little different.

Maybe it is my imagination? she thought. But when she went back to her bedroom, she was sure.

My suitcase is open. I know I shut it before I went out. And my backpack is on the bed. I know I left it on the side table! Shall I go and tell Clara? Shall I call the police? No. There is no one here now. What can they do? I know that nothing of mine has been stolen. And my great-uncle's things...? Well I don't know.

Beth went around the house again. She checked every window and the front and back doors. Then she went to bed.

17. SIGHTSEEING

The next morning Beth woke up early. The hot dry wind had stopped and the sun was shining. It was a beautiful day. Beth opened all the windows to let the fresh air and sunlight into the house.

I'm going to ride a bike today, she thought. So she dressed in shorts and a bright green T-shirt. She ate breakfast in the kitchen. After tidying her bedroom and the kitchen, she went into the living room to read for a while, but she couldn't concentrate on her book.

Who came into the house last night? What did they want? Did they steal something from the house?

At 11:00am, Tim arrived.

"I have my car today," he said. "We'll drive to my flat and collect my sister's bicycle."

He came into the house while Beth took her backpack, and put her handbag and iPad inside it. Beth closed all the windows and checked the front door. They went outside and she locked the back door.

"You are very careful," said Tim. "Do you think someone will break into the house?"

They walked out to the road and got into Tim's car. As Tim drove towards the city, Beth explained.

"I am sure someone came into the house yesterday. I didn't lock the back door when I went to visit Clara. I locked it later. Maybe someone was inside. When I came back to the house last night my bedroom window was open. Someone had moved things in my bedroom and I thought the other rooms looked different. Maybe someone was looking for something."

"Was anything missing?" asked Tim.

"Nothing of mine is missing, but I don't know about Great-Uncle William's things. Maybe you can look later."

"Sure" said Tim. "I can look, but I am worried about you."

Tim lived on the top floor of an old house near the university. He parked his car behind the house.

"Why don't we eat lunch first?" he said.

He took Beth to a small café. They ordered salads and fruit juice and then found a table in the garden behind the café. Beth looked around. It was a pretty garden with a small pond and a fountain. The sun was shining and the sky was bright blue with fluffy white clouds.

"I love it here," said Beth. "I should be sad about Great-Uncle William. But today I feel happy. Christchurch is very nice."

"Why don't you relax for the afternoon?" said Tim. "I know you have many questions. But forget about them for the afternoon. Enjoy Christchurch."

After they had eaten, Tim said, "Sightseeing by bicycle. It is the best way. I will take you on a tour."

Beth was surprised. "Don't you have to work?"

"I often work very late and on weekends. So my boss thinks it's OK if I take a day off sometimes."

They went back to Tim's flat. He took his sister's bicycle and a cycling helmet out of the shed. "Here you are."

"Are you sure your sister won't mind?"

"I emailed her last night. She said 'no problem'. Do you have sun block?"

"Sun block?"

"Yes, sun block. Even when it is not very hot, the sun is strong here. I'll get you some." Tim disappeared up a flight of stairs on the outside of the house. He returned quickly with a tube of sun block. "Use this," he said.

Beth enjoyed the afternoon very much. They cycled along the Avon River. They went to see the cardboard cathedral.

"The main cathedral in the city was damaged in the big earthquake," said Tim. "This is a temporary one. It was designed by a famous Japanese architect. I like it very much." After visiting the cardboard cathedral, they cycled through the Botanical Gardens.

At 4:30, Tim said, "You must be hot and tired. Shall we go back to Fendalton? I will look to see if anything was stolen yesterday."

"Thank you. Yes, I am a bit tired."

Back at Great-Uncle William's house, Beth took a shower, while Tim looked through the house. He was sitting in the kitchen drinking water, when Beth came back. She was wearing a cornflower blue sundress and her hair was tied up on top of her head.

"Wow! You look stunning!" said Tim.

"Thank you," said Beth. *Shall I tell him I made this dress from some second-hand curtains? Maybe not.*

"I can't find anything missing," he said. "Of course someone might have taken some papers or books. I don't know. The cabinets and desk drawers are all locked, but there are a lot of papers lying around."

Beth got a glass of water and sat down at the table.

"Are there any restaurants around here that deliver meals?"

"Yes. There are a lot of pizza places near here and a very good Thai takeaway."

"Oh, good! Thai. I love Thai food and I'm very hungry. Will you stay and have dinner with me?"

"Sure," said Tim.

"Maybe we can ask Clara too," said Beth.

"Good idea," said Tim. "Call her. She gave me her phone number last night."

He found Clara's number on his phone and handed it to Beth.

Beth talked to Clara. "She said she would love to come," she told Tim. "But tonight she has choir practice. So she can't."

"OK," said Tim. "Thai food for two."

Tim found the restaurant menu on his smartphone and they chose some food. Tim called and gave their order. "They're busy. It will be here in an hour. Is that OK?"

"Sure," said Beth. "I wonder if we can find anything to drink."

Tim looked through the cupboards in the kitchen. He found some cans of beer and put them in the refrigerator. He chose a bottle of wine from the wine rack in the kitchen, and opened it.

"Why don't we go into the living room?" said Beth. "I have something I want to show you."

Beth opened all the windows in the living room. She sat down on the sofa and took her great-uncle's letter out of her handbag. She handed it to Tim.

"Read this," she said.

18. SILAS FEELS LUCKY

Silas had a bad day. He got up early. He planned to watch the house. He didn't know how to find the treasure in the house. He thought maybe it wasn't there. Maybe Beth and her great-uncle would go somewhere to get it. So when they went out, he would follow them.

He was waiting opposite the house in Fendalton when Tim arrived.

Who is that? he wondered. Then Beth came out with Tim and they drove away.

This is bad luck, thought Silas. *I can't follow them. I will have to get some transport. A motorbike would be good.*

Silas went to a pub. He found a man in the pub who looked a little like him. He waited for his chance and stole the man's wallet. He went to a hire shop and used the credit card and driver's license from the wallet to hire a motorbike.

He rode back to the house in Fendalton. He waited for a while on the street near the house, but he got bored and tired. Also, he thought people would notice him if he stayed on the street too long.

He parked the motorbike outside the local bank and walked back to the house. He went into the garden and around to the side of the house. He lay down on the ground under the windows.

I'll wait here until Beth comes back, he thought. *I wonder where her great-uncle is. I haven't seen him yet.*

The sun was hot and Silas was tired. He fell asleep.

The sound of people talking woke him up. It was early evening.

The windows above his head were open. It was Beth and a man. Silas thought it was a young man's voice. Maybe it was the young man who came in the car this morning.

They were talking about the letter. They were talking about the treasure! He could hear every word.

This is lucky, thought Silas. *I will find out everything.*

19. A MYSTERY

Tim read Great-Uncle William's letter.

"---'*I have many things to tell you and a treasure to give you. It is very valuable*'--- . I don't know what he means," said Tim.

"Neither do I," said Beth. "Did he have a lot of money?"

"I don't know," said Tim. "He lived a comfortable life, but look at this house. It is not the house of a rich man."

"He knew a lot about paintings, didn't he?" Beth pointed to the paintings on the walls of the living room. "Are these very valuable?"

"They are good, and some of them are very old. I like them a lot. But they are not so valuable. Maybe all together they are worth a hundred thousand dollars."

Outside the house, Silas was excited. *A hundred thousand dollars! I'll take those paintings. I wonder where I can sell them.*

Inside the house, Beth was amazed. "A hundred thousand dollars! That's a lot of money!"

Tim smiled at her. "Well, yes. I guess it is a lot of money, but the Professor wrote 'a treasure'. I don't think he meant those pictures. And he wrote about a secret. Those pictures are hanging on the wall. They are not a secret."

"What did you talk about when you came to visit him?" asked Beth.

"In the beginning, he helped me with my work. Some of the paintings in the basement of the museum are very old. Your great-uncle's specialty was fifteenth and sixteenth century Italian art. The paintings in the basement of the museum are not as old as that, but they came from Europe. He helped me to identify artists and helped me to decide how to clean and repair the paintings.

"After Christmas, when he became ill, he often asked me to help him. He became very worried about his papers and the files on his computer. He asked me to put a password on his computer, so that no one could read his files. He wouldn't send emails any more. He said that it was dangerous. He believed that his computer might be hacked. He was very ill and very nervous."

"Oh," said Beth. "Now I understand why he wrote me a letter. At first I thought he was a very old man. I thought he didn't have a computer. I thought he didn't know how to use email. When I saw the computer in his office, I was very surprised."

Tim poured them both another glass of wine. "Oh, the Professor could use a computer. He didn't know much about computer security, but he always used a computer to send emails to researchers in other countries. He had many contacts in Europe. He always wrote his reports on the computer too. Maybe we will find the answer to the mystery on his computer. He was so worried about the files on it. Maybe we should go and look at his files."

"But the computer has password protection," said Beth. "We can't read his files."

Tim stood up. "You forgot. I put the password protection on the computer for him. So I know what the password is! Let's go and look!"

They left the living room and went into the office.

Outside Silas was angry.

I'll have to go around to the other side of the house, he thought. *I hope the windows are open.*

Silas walked around the back of the house and down the driveway on the other side. He knelt down under the side window of the office. He was lucky. The room was hot, and Beth had opened the windows. Once again, he could hear what they were saying.

Tim was sitting at the computer. He turned it on.

"The password is Brush2stroke," he said. He entered the password. "What shall we look for?" he asked Beth.

"Uh, maybe we should look at the most recent files. It was only after Christmas that Great-Uncle William became worried and nervous. Maybe he wrote something then."

Tim searched the files. "Here we are, he said. The most recent activity is a file called 'Confession'. It's locked. We need another password. I showed the Professor how to do it. He must have protected this folder himself."

"Oh, no!" said Beth. "Now we will never know what he wrote."

Tim looked at Beth. She was standing by the window. He thought she was very beautiful.

I like Beth very much, he thought. *I think I am falling in love with her.*

He stared at the computer screen. *I wonder what password he used.*

Then he had an idea. He typed in b-e-t-h, and the folder opened.

"Come and look," he told Beth. "The password for the file was your name. I am sure the Professor wanted you to read this."

Beth brought another chair and sat down next to Tim. They read the file together.

20. CONFESSION

---My dear Beth,

If you are reading this, then I am dead. I wanted to tell you the story myself, but I am worried I will die before I have the chance. So I am writing everything down. It is very important that you understand.

I don't know how much you have learned about your father's family. So I will tell you the important things. My father was called George. He was in the army. After the Second World War, he married, bought a house in Dumfries in Scotland, and had two sons. I was the elder son and my younger brother, Alan, was your grandfather. My father was a businessman, but he also liked farming. He bought a farm called Hill Top near Dumfries. He wanted me to become a farmer, but I was not interested. Luckily, Alan was interested in farming, so the plan was that Alan would take over the farm. I was interested in languages and art. I studied at university and I hoped to become an art historian. Everything was fine until 1960.

In 1960, my father had problems with his business. He needed a lot of money to save his company. He could have sold Hill Top farm, but he wanted to keep it for Alan. He called me home from university. He told me he wanted my help. He opened a secret cupboard in his office. He took out a square package. He said, "I got this during the war. I want to sell it to save the company. You know about the art world. Where can I sell it? How much money can I get?"

I opened the package. Inside was a painting of the Virgin Mary. It was very, very old. The surprising thing was that I knew the painting. At university I did a course on missing art treasures. I had seen pictures of this painting. "You can't sell this!" I told my father. "This is on the lists of art treasures that were stolen during the Second World War. Where did you get it?"

"Oh, I found it during the war. We were hiding in a church in Italy. I found it hidden behind the altar. I took it as a souvenir. Later, I thought it might be valuable, so I kept it."

"You stole it!" I told my father. "If you take this to an auction house or an art dealer, everyone will know you stole it. You will be in a lot of trouble."

"It's mine," said my father. "If I can't sell it to an art dealer, I will sell it to a private buyer. There are always people who will buy treasures. I guess it is worth a lot of money."

I argued with my father. I told him he must give the painting back. I talked to Alan, my brother. "Tell Father to sell the farm. Then he will have enough money to save his company." But Alan wouldn't listen to me. He wanted our father to keep the farm, because our father planned to give it to him.

There was a terrible argument. That night I took the painting from my father's office. I went to London. I took all the money I had in the bank, and I sold everything I owned. I had enough money to go to America. I went to America and I took the painting with me. I thought my father would sell the farm. But he didn't. He kept the farm but he lost his company. I never spoke to my father or brother again.

I thought I could give the painting back but it was difficult. The people who were hunting for the stolen treasures from the Second World War wanted the treasures back. But they also wanted to find the people who stole them. They wanted to punish the thieves. I still loved my father, and I didn't want him to be in trouble.

I thought I would wait. I thought that after a few years, no one would ask any questions. But in fact, the people kept looking for the thieves and looking for the treasures. The painting my father stole was always high on the list of 'most wanted treasures'.

I got a job in America and I worked hard. When I had enough money, I studied at a university in Chicago. I was successful. I got a job in an important museum. I became quite famous as an art expert.

Of course, then it was impossible to give the painting back. I would lose my job if anyone knew I had been hiding this precious painting for so many years. I was always worried. I was always frightened that someone would find out my secret.

Then one day, I read a report about the painting. Someone did some very good detective work. They found out that at the time the painting was stolen, there were British soldiers hiding in the church. The report said that maybe one of the soldiers had stolen the painting. The treasure hunters were trying to find out the names of the soldiers.

I panicked. I gave up my job and moved to New Zealand. I brought the painting with me.

I am not proud of what I did. I am very ashamed. I hope you will understand. I know I am dying. I am leaving everything I own to you. Of course this means that you will also have the painting. My father is dead and so is my brother. Your father is dead. So no one will be in trouble if you give the painting back now. I hope you will do this for me. Contact Tim Gaskell at the Christchurch museum. He is a very nice man and he is very clever. He will help you.

I wish we had met. I am sure I would have loved you very much.
Your loving great-uncle,
William Whitley-Sneddon ---

21. WHAT SHALL WE DO?

Beth and Tim didn't talk while they were reading the letter. When they finished, they stared at each other.

Outside the window, Silas was still waiting for them to speak, but there was no sound coming from the office.

"Hey, you!" shouted a voice. "What are you doing?"

Silas jumped up. It was the deliveryman from the Thai restaurant. "Get away from that window!" shouted the man. "I'll call the police! I'll tell the people inside about you!"

Silas ran down the driveway. He knocked the deliveryman to the ground. Then he ran through the gate and down the road.

Beth and Tim heard the shouting. They unlocked the front door and ran outside. The deliveryman was getting off the ground. He was picking up the boxes of Thai food. There was no sign of Silas.

"Oh dear! What happened?" asked Beth, running to help the deliveryman. "Did you fall over?"

"I was pushed over," answered the man. "Some guy was kneeling under that window, listening. When I shouted at him, he pushed me over and ran away. I think you have a problem. I think you should call the police!"

Tim ran out to the road and looked. He came back. "I can't see anyone."

"Well, I think you should call the police," said the deliveryman.

"Are you OK?" Beth asked him.

"Yes, I'm OK."

The deliveryman gave the boxes of food to Tim, and Beth paid him.

"Thanks. I hope your food is OK."

Tim and Beth went back inside. Beth ran into the living room and the office and closed all the windows. She was shivering.

"Someone was outside listening to us! It makes me feel frightened. Who was it?"

"I don't know," said Tim. He hugged Beth. "Try not to worry. Why don't you put the food on the table? I'm going outside."

Beth found plates and knives and forks. She put glasses on the table and took the beer out of the refrigerator.

Tim came in and sat down. "The grass under the side window of the living room is flat. It looks like someone was lying there. I guess that guy was listening to us talking in the living room. Then when we moved to the office, he moved too."

"Why?"

"I wish I knew," answered Tim. "Anyway, let's eat. Our food is getting cold."

After dinner, Beth and Tim tidied up and washed the dishes. Beth didn't want to go to the front of the house, so they stayed in the kitchen.

"Tim," said Beth. "What do you think about the letter? Were you surprised?"

"Yes," said Tim. "I was very surprised. But I think I understand how it happened. Poor Professor. It must have been very difficult for him."

"The letter doesn't say what the picture is," said Beth.

"No," answered Tim. "But I think I can guess. The Professor gave us some clues. It was a painting of the Virgin Mary. It was very old. Your great-grandfather stole it from a church in Italy. If my guess is right, that painting is worth millions of dollars."

"What! And it's somewhere in this house!"

"We don't know where it is," said Tim. "So we have to find it. Then we have to give it back. Unless you want to keep it?"

"Of course not!" said Beth. "Are you crazy?"

Tim laughed. "I was just joking." Then Tim was very serious. "I am thinking about the man who was listening at the window. I guess it was the same person who came into the house yesterday. We can call the police, but I don't know what we can tell them. We don't think anything was stolen. Maybe they will ask the local patrol car to drive past the house, but I think that will be all."

"We could tell them there's a painting worth millions of dollars in the house," said Beth.

"Yes, maybe. But they would tell us to call an insurance company and get an alarm system. Or to take the painting to the museum. We don't know where it is. Maybe it is not in the house. The Professor might have hidden it somewhere else.

"But I am going to stay with you tonight. I will stay awake. Maybe the man will come back."

"Thank you," said Beth. "I would like that."

"I'll go back to my flat and get some clothes. I won't be away long."

Tim went out of the back door and Beth locked it. She went around the house and closed all the curtains. Then she sat at the kitchen table and waited for Tim.

He came back with a backpack and a supermarket bag.

"I left my bicycle at the flat and came back by car. I got something for breakfast. Were you OK while I was gone?"

"Yes. Nothing happened, but I'm pleased you're back."

22. NO LUCK

Beth went to bed early. She was very tired, but it took her a long time to fall asleep. So much had happened. She thought about Great-Uncle William's will.

I own this house, she thought. She thought about Great-Uncle William's letter. But mostly she thought about Tim. *He is so nice! I feel very safe when he is here. And he is very good looking. I will be sorry when I leave and go back to Manchester. I wonder if he ever travels to England.*

Finally Beth fell asleep.

Tim checked all the doors and windows and turned out the lights. He sat in the living room. He waited and watched. He did not feel sleepy.

I can't believe it! he thought. *The missing Rubens. The one that disappeared from the church in northern Italy in nineteen forty-four might be here! In this house! Or maybe the Professor hid it somewhere else. Beth and I will have to start searching tomorrow. I will call my boss and tell him I am on the hunt for an important painting. I am sure he will let me have some free time.*

And then, he thought, *Beth has come into my life. I never thought I would meet a girl like her. I wonder what she thinks of me. Does she have a boyfriend in England? Can I ask her?*

A few kilometres away, Silas was drinking in a pub. He was worried.

The deliveryman saw me, he thought. *I will have to be careful. I can go back and steal those pictures from the house. That man said they were worth about a hundred thousand dollars. But it seems that there is something more valuable. I wonder what it is. I wonder where it is. I can't listen outside the house again, but maybe I can follow them. I have the motorbike now. So I'll wait near the house tomorrow until they go out.*

23. WHERE IS THE PAINTING?

The next morning, Beth got up very early. She found Tim in an armchair in the living room.

He looked very tired, but he smiled at her. "It was very quiet. No visitors!"

Beth made breakfast. Then she said, "Go and have some sleep. I am perfectly OK."

"Are you sure?"

"Yes. I slept well and the sun is shining. I will do some laundry and I will send emails to my friend Penny and my mother. I don't feel frightened or worried this morning."

"Promise me you will come and wake me up if you see anyone. And don't answer the door!"

"I promise. I'll only open it for Clara."

Tim lay down on the bed in Great-Uncle William's room.

As he fell asleep, he thought, *Beth will email her friend and her mother. She didn't say anything about a boyfriend. That's good.*

When Tim woke up, it was almost lunchtime. Across the road, Silas was pretending to work on his motorbike. He was getting bored and angry. People in cars stopped to ask if they could help him. People walking along the footpath stopped to chat to him and watch what he was doing.

Beth made coffee for Tim. "There's nothing much to eat. I'm sorry."

"That's OK. I can go down to the supermarket and get something. But for now, coffee is all I need. We have to make a plan. We have to find the painting."

"Yes, I've been thinking about that," said Beth. "I think I will call the lawyer. Maybe Great-Uncle William left a letter for me. And I think we should search the house."

"I agree. I'll go down to the supermarket. I'll leave my mobile phone with you. You can call the lawyer and if anything strange happens, you can call the police. I'll only be gone about twenty-five minutes."

Tim drove down to the supermarket while Beth made the phone call.

Silas saw Tim get into his car and drive down the road, but he didn't follow him.

Beth is the important one, he thought. *I have to follow her, wherever she goes.*

When Tim got back, she was still talking on the phone.

"Yes, Mr Pringle. I understand. ....Yes, I will tell you as soon as I decide about the house......... Yes I will come and see you before the end of the week. Thank you, Goodbye."

Beth gave the telephone back to Tim. "I talked for a long time. It probably cost a lot. I'm sorry."

"That's OK." Tim smiled. "Did the lawyer know anything? Does he have a letter for you?"

"His name is Ivan Pringle. I didn't say anything about the missing painting or the computer file we found. I just asked if there were any letters or messages for me. He said there wasn't anything. But they have almost finished all the paperwork. The most important thing I want to tell you is that Mr Pringle has written you a letter."

"A letter to me? Why?"

"Well Great-Uncle William wanted you to have all the paintings in the house. Except one. It is a painting he did himself. It is of the house in Dumfries where he grew up. He wanted me to have that. The others are yours. Mr Pringle said that they are insured for a hundred and fifty thousand dollars."

"I can't believe it," said Tim. "But I feel that you should have them. If you don't want to keep them, you could sell them. I'm sure the money would be useful for you."

"No, Tim," said Beth. "They are yours. Great-Uncle William wanted you to have them."

Beth didn't tell Tim the other surprising thing she had heard from the lawyer.

...'Your great uncle had a good job, but he had a very simple lifestyle. He saved a lot of money. Between investments and money in the bank, he left about one and a half million dollars. And his house is small, but it has a big garden and the location is very good. I think you could sell the house for about six hundred thousand dollars.' ...

Beth felt strange about this news. She had never had much money. Now it seemed she had a lot of money.

I suppose I will get used to the idea, she thought. *And I will be able to give some money to my mother.*

After lunch, Tim and Beth searched the house. They looked everywhere. They emptied every cupboard and cabinet. They lifted carpets and looked at the floorboards. Tim climbed into the space between the roof and the ceiling. They found the keys for the desk drawers and filing cabinets under Great-Uncle William's mattress. They searched through all the papers in the drawers and cabinets. They took all the books off the bookshelves. They found nothing. No painting, and they had no idea where to look.

While they were doing this, Silas was still watching the house. At 4:00pm he gave up. He was hungry. He was also bored and angry.

I give up. I will get into the house and take those paintings from the living room. They are worth a hundred thousand dollars. That's enough. I have to find a way to get them out.

Silas thought hard. Then he had an idea. He thought it was a very good idea.

It will be better to do it after it gets dark, he thought. *I'll go and eat and get some supplies. I'll come back here later.*

Tim and Beth stopped and ate sandwiches at 7:00pm. Then they kept on searching. By 10:00pm they were both dirty and very, very tired.

"I give up," said Beth. "I don't know where else to look."

"I don't know either," said Tim. "Let's stop. Let's drink some wine and relax."

They sat in the living room. Tim looked at the pictures on the walls.

"You are sure the lawyer said these are mine?" he asked Beth.

"Yes, I'm sure. The lawyer said all the paintings in the house except one. So yes, these are yours."

Tim took the paintings down and looked at them under the light.

"I am so pleased to have these. They are not by famous artists but they are very good. I think they are worth more than a hundred and fifty thousand dollars. But I would never sell them."

He hung them back on the walls.

"I'm glad you like them." Beth smiled.

"And what about your painting? The one of the house in Dumfries? Where is that?"

"I saw it in Great-Uncle William's bedroom. It's hanging above his bed."

"Let's have a look at it. Shall I bring it in here?" asked Tim.

"Yes, please. I don't think it's very good, but I'm pleased to have it."

While Tim was collecting the painting from the bedroom, Silas arrived on his motorbike and parked it out on the street. He had a big canvas bag and a backpack. He hid the big bag near the front door of the house. Then he went next door to Clara's house. There were no lights on.

Whoever lives here is probably in bed, thought Silas.

He went behind Clara's garden shed. He took a can of petrol, a container of oil, some old cloths and two bottles out of his backpack. He put the petrol in the bottles. He soaked the cloths in oil and pushed them in the top of the bottles.

Good, he thought. *I'm ready. I'm sure my idea will work. Now where will be the best place to use them?*

Tim came back into the living room. He was carrying the picture. He put it down on the coffee table.

"The painting's not so bad," he said. "The frame's strange though. It looks like the professor made it himself. See, it's more like a box than a picture frame…"

Just then there was a very loud bang, and then another one.

"What's that?" Beth ran to the front door and opened it. "It came from Clara's! Tim! Clara's house is burning!"

She ran out of the door and Tim ran after her. He gave Beth his phone.

"Dial 111! Get the emergency services! Fire brigade and ambulance! Clara might be in the house!"

Beth made the call and then followed Tim. People were running out of houses along the street. Everyone was shouting and pointing at the house. No one saw Silas climb over the fence from Clara's back garden.

Tim broke the glass in the front door and opened it. He went into the house to look for Clara. Beth was terrified.

He came out of the house just as the fire engines arrived. His face was black and he was coughing.

"I don't think she's at home. I think the house is empty. Most of the fire is at the back of the house," he told the firemen.

Beth held tight to Tim. "I was so frightened when you went into the house."

Then they saw Clara standing in the garden. Beth ran to her and hugged her.

"Oh, Clara! Thank goodness! We thought you were in the house!"

"I was visiting some friends down the road. We heard the noise and came out to see what it was. My poor house!" Clara was crying.

Clara's friends gathered around her.

"We can't do anything here," said Tim. "Clara's safe. Her friends will look after her. Let's go back to the house."

He took Beth's hand and they started walking back.

Silas was still in the living room. He was packing the paintings from the living room into the big canvas bag. He knew that they were valuable, so he had brought bubble wrap to protect them. He had finished packing when he saw the painting on the coffee table, so he put that on top. He was very pleased with himself.

I'm smart. They are worrying about the fire next door. They left the door open for me.

Silas walked out the front door carrying the bag. He was walking down the path when Beth and Tim saw him.

"Hey, you!" shouted Beth. Usually Beth was very quiet and gentle, but everything that had happened, and especially the fire in Clara's house, made her very angry. She dropped Tim's hand and ran towards Silas.

"What are you doing? What are you taking from the house?"

Silas had a knife in his pocket. He dropped the bag and tried to get his knife out, but Beth was too quick. She jumped on Silas. She was shouting and hitting him. Silas was very surprised. He pushed Beth to the ground. He ran down the path and jumped on his motorbike. He rode away.

Tim helped Beth to stand up. He was very kind to Beth, but he was also laughing.

"Are you mad?" he asked. "Is the woman I love crazy?"

He picked up the bag and put his other arm around Beth. "Let's go inside," he said.

They went back into the house and into the living room. Beth sat down on the sofa and Tim put the bag on the floor.

"I need a glass of water," he said. "And I need to wash."

When Tim came back, Beth was asleep. Tim went to her bedroom and found a blanket. He put the blanket over Beth. He looked at the walls of the living room. All the paintings were gone.

I guess they are in this bag, he thought. *It doesn't matter. I am too tired to think about anything. We will talk to the police tomorrow. But now I need to sleep.*

He locked the house doors, went to Great-Uncle William's bedroom, and threw himself on the bed. Seconds later, he was asleep.

24. THE NEXT DAY

Beth was surprised when she woke up the next morning.
Why am I here on the sofa? Where's Tim?
She thought about everything that happened the night before. *Did Tim really say 'the woman I love'? Or did I imagine it?*
Beth felt very happy, but then she remembered Clara.
Poor Clara. What a terrible thing to happen! I wonder how she is feeling this morning.
Beth went to the kitchen and made coffee. She stared out of the kitchen window while she drank her coffee. The back of Clara's house was completely burnt out.
Imagine if Clara had been in her house last night! She might have died! I wonder what caused the fire. There were two big bangs before the fire started. Was it a gas explosion?
She finished her coffee and went to her bedroom to get some clothes. The door to Great-Uncle Williams bedroom was half open. Beth looked in. Tim was lying on top of the bed. He was still asleep. Very quietly, Beth closed the door.
By the time Beth had showered and washed her hair, Tim was up. She found him in the kitchen, drinking coffee.
"Do you want some toast?" he asked.
"Yes. I'm starving. But I'll make it."
"OK. I'll go and take a shower. I smell of smoke!"
After breakfast, Beth went back into the living room. The big canvas bag was still on the floor. Tim joined her there.
"I'll check the paintings," he said. "I hope they weren't damaged

when that guy dropped the bag."

He opened the bag and took out the painting of the house in Dumfries.

"Oh. This is damaged. Look. The frame is cracked. It's a very strange picture frame. You should take it to a shop and get another one………" Tim stopped talking. He was holding the picture frame in his hands and staring at it.

"What is it?" asked Beth.

At that moment, they heard the sound of the front gate opening. A policeman was walking down the path towards the house. Very quickly Tim put the picture he was holding under the sofa. He looked at Beth.

"Don't say anything about that picture," he said.

Beth went to the door and invited the policeman in.

The policeman came into the living room and sat down.

"We found out that the fire next door was not an accident," said the policeman. "Someone threw two petrol bombs at the house. I want to know if you heard or saw anything."

Tim and Beth told the policeman about the loud bangs. They explained they ran out of the house and that Tim went into Clara's house to rescue her. But Clara wasn't there.

"Thank you," said the policeman. "But we don't know why someone wanted to attack Mrs Bolton. Do you have any ideas?"

"Yes, I do," said Tim. "I think I know why someone set fire to her house."

He pointed to the bag on the floor.

"Three days ago, someone came into this house. The backdoor was unlocked because Beth was next door with Clara Bolton. Beth came back, and locked the backdoor before she went into the city. She didn't come into the house but I think someone was inside. When Beth came back later, the window in her bedroom was open. She knows it was shut when she went out."

"Is this true?" the policeman asked Beth.

"Yes, that's right," answered Beth. "I could see that things in the house had been moved but nothing was missing, so I didn't call the police."

"Then the day before yesterday, a delivery man came here. He saw a man sitting under an open window listening to Beth and me talking. The deliveryman shouted and the other man ran away," said Tim.

"When I went out to look, I found that someone had been lying on the ground outside the windows of this room too."

"But you didn't see this man," said the policeman.

"No, not then," said Tim. "But I think we saw him last night. I guess it was the same man."

Beth explained about walking back from the fire. "We saw a man walking from the front door of this house. He was carrying this bag."

She pointed to the bag of paintings.

"I shouted at him and pushed him. He dropped the bag and ran away. He left on a motorbike."

"So I think the man started the fire at Clara's house so that we would go out of this house. Then he came in to steal the paintings," said Tim.

"Paintings?" said the policeman. "This bag is full of paintings?"

"Yes. They belonged to my great-uncle. This was his house. He died and left the paintings to Tim."

"We were talking about them in this room," said Tim. "We were talking about their value. I think the man was lying outside the window. He heard that they were worth a hundred thousand dollars or more. I think he decided to steal them."

"It is a good story," said the policeman. "But why was he there? Why did he come to search the house? And why was he lying outside the window listening?"

"I don't know," said Tim.

"My great-uncle just died," said Beth. "Maybe he thought the house would be empty. Maybe he thought there would be money in the house."

"Maybe that's true," said the policeman. "I will take this bag of paintings back to the police station. Our experts will look for fingerprints."

"OK," said Tim. "But please be careful. I want them back. They are very nice paintings!"

The policeman wrote a receipt for Tim and went away.

Tim watched him walk down the path and get into the police car. Then he turned to Beth. He looked very excited.

"I've found the missing painting!"

"Where?" Beth was amazed.

Tim knelt on the floor and took the painting in its strange box frame out from under the sofa. He put it on the coffee table. He pointed to the crack in the frame.

"There is a second painting inside. It is hidden behind the other one! I am sure it is the missing treasure!"

"Oh!" said Beth. "What shall we do?"

"I don't want to take it out here. I might damage it. I want to take it to my workshop at the museum. Is that OK?"

"Of course," said Beth.

"Will you come with me?" asked Tim.

"No. I want to go and see Clara. I want to see if I can help her."

"If the missing painting is inside this frame, I will have to ask for some help and some advice. Do you mind if I tell someone else about it?"

"No, that's OK. It was Great-Uncle William's secret. But he wanted me to give the painting back. I can't give it back without telling people about what happened. It can't hurt Great-Uncle William now. He's dead."

"Are you sure?" asked Tim.

"Yes, I'm sure. Great-Uncle William wrote that you would help me. I don't know how to give the painting back. So I am hoping you will do everything."

Tim pulled Beth to her feet and kissed her.

"Finding the painting is wonderful. But meeting you is the best thing that ever happened to me."

25. TIM TALKS TO HIS BOSS

Tim drove to the museum and carefully carried the painting down to the workshop in the basement. His friend Kenny, who worked on fossils, was busy cleaning a giant clam.

"Where have you been?" asked Kenny. "I haven't seen you for days!"

"I've been treasure hunting," answered Tim.

"Oh yeah." Kenny laughed. "I think you've been sunbathing and drinking beer!"

"Kenny, will you stop what you're doing and help me?"

"Sure. What can I do?"

"Lock the door and come with me to the clean room. I want to open a frame and I have to be very careful."

Kenny helped Tim take the box frame apart. Tim put the painting of the house on a side table. Then he lifted some layers of paper and wood and saw the painting underneath. He stared and stared.

Kenny looked at his friend.

"You are very pale, Tim," he said. "Are you OK? What is it?"

"This," said Tim. "This is the missing Rubens Virgin. It disappeared from a church in Italy in nineteen forty-two. People have been looking for it for more than seventy years."

"Wow," said Kenny. "I wonder if it's worth more than my giant clam."

"Stay here Kenny! Lock the door behind me. Don't leave the workshop. I'm going upstairs."

Tim ran up the stairs to the Art Director's office. He was lucky.

His boss was sitting reading a report.

He knocked and walked into the office.

"Oh, there you are Tim," said his boss. "I wondered when you were coming back to work."

Tim shut the door and turned to his boss.

"I have something to tell you," he said.

26. WE ARE LOOKING FOR THE THIEF

Beth went next door to Clara's house. The fire department officers were still working there. They were searching for clues about the fire. She asked them how to find Clara.

"She is with her friend down the road," said one of the workers. "It's the blue house with the big garage in front."

Beth walked down the road, found the house and knocked. Clara's friend came to the door and Beth introduced herself.

"I am worrying about Clara," she said. "Can I talk with her?"

"Yes," answered the woman. "Of course. Come in."

Clara was sitting in the kitchen.

"Oh, Beth," she said. "Thank you for coming. Are you and Tim OK?"

"Yes. We're fine," answered Beth. "How about you?"

"I'm feeling better today," said Clara. "The kitchen and bathroom are destroyed, but most of the front of the house is OK. The insurance company will pay to rebuild my house. Most of my personal treasures were in the front rooms so I haven't lost any photographs or things like that. I was lucky."

"I am so pleased," said Beth. "I have been worried about you."

Beth chatted to Clara and her friend for a few minutes. Then she walked to the supermarket to buy food. It was a nice day and she enjoyed the long walk.

There has been too much excitement and drama, she thought. *I need some quiet time to think about everything.*

When she got to Great-Uncle William's house, a police car was

The Legacy

parked outside. The policeman who had visited her that morning got out.

"I've been waiting for you," he said. "I have to talk to you, and of course, I couldn't call you."

"No," said Beth. "Sorry. My great-uncle didn't have a telephone and I have only been in New Zealand a few days. I haven't organized a mobile phone yet."

"Can I come into the house?" asked the policeman.

"Of course," answered Beth.

Beth took the policeman into the kitchen. She was hot and thirsty.

"Would you like something to drink?" she asked the policeman.

"No. I'm fine, thank you," he answered. "But you go ahead."

Beth got a glass of water and sat down.

"We found fingerprints on those paintings in the bag," said the policeman. "We didn't have any records for those fingerprints in New Zealand so we searched the international database. We found a record for them. They belong to an Englishman. The English police are looking for him because he murdered a man outside a pub."

"But why was he here? Why did he come to this house?"

"I wonder if you know him. He is English. Maybe you met him in England. His name is Silas Rottle."

Beth was very surprised. "I never met anyone called Silas Rottle. But just before I came here, I got a new flatmate. Her name is Margot Rottle."

"Did you tell her about this house? Did you tell her about Professor Whitley-Sneddon's paintings?"

"No. I didn't like her. I didn't tell her anything. But she was always reading my letters, and searching my room. I guess she could have found out."

"She doesn't sound like a very nice flatmate," said the policeman.

"No. I moved out of the flat before I came here."

"We will talk to the English police. Can you give me any more information about her?"

Beth gave the policeman the address of the flat and the name of the company where Margot worked.

"We checked all the airline passengers. We know Silas Rottle is still in New Zealand. We are looking for him. We will find him. But until we find him, you must be careful. He is a dangerous and violent person."

"Do you think he will come back to this house?" Beth was frightened.

"I don't think so. But maybe. So I think you should go and stay in a hotel until we find him. Why don't you pack a bag? I will drive you to a nice quiet hotel. You will be safe there."

"But what about Tim?" asked Beth. "Tim said he would come back here. He is at the museum now. He works there."

"I'll call the museum and talk to Mr Gaskell. I will tell him where you are staying. He can call you at the hotel," said the policeman.

The policeman took Beth to a small hotel. It was next to the River Avon.

Tim and I cycled along that river, thought Beth. *I hope we can do it again sometime.*

Beth stayed in her hotel room. She was waiting for Tim to call her. It was quite late when he called.

"How is Clara?" he asked. "Is she OK?"

"Yes. I saw her. She seemed OK. But tell me, what happened? The painting hidden in the frame. Was it the right one?"

"Yes," said Tim. "My guess was right. It has been a very busy and exciting day. I still have a lot to do. Will you be OK tonight? I don't think I have time to come to see you."

"Yes, of course I will be OK. But when will I see you?"

"Tomorrow. Tomorrow at lunchtime. I will come and pick you up from the hotel. We are going to Wellington."

"Wellington! Why?"

"It's a surprise. Pack clothes for two days. You will need a formal day dress to wear tomorrow, and something very glamorous for the evening."

"But, Tim…"

"Sorry. I have to go. Tomorrow at twelve-thirty. See you then."

Beth felt irritated. She was sure that she was falling in love with Tim but men were sometimes very annoying. She looked at the clothes in her bag.

I packed for a summer vacation, she thought. *I don't have the right clothes. I will have to go shopping tomorrow.*

The next morning, Beth asked the young woman at the front desk of the hotel about dress shops.

"I like Chelsea," said the receptionist. "They have lovely clothes. But they are very expensive."

The Legacy

"Where is it?" asked Beth. "Is it far?"

"No. It's only about a ten-minute walk. I'll show you on the map."

Beth was nervous. *That man Silas Rottle is in the city somewhere,* she thought. *I don't want to walk anywhere alone.*

"I think I'll take a taxi," she told the receptionist. "Can you call one for me, please?"

The taxi stopped outside Chelsea. Beth went inside and looked at the clothes. They were beautiful. But the receptionist was correct. They were very expensive.

I have money now, thought Beth. *I can buy expensive clothes.*

She bought two dresses. One was blue. It was very simple and elegant. The other dress was green. It had narrow shoulder straps and was decorated with beads. The shop sold shoes and handbags too. Beth bought blue shoes and a handbag to match the blue dress. Then she found gold sandals and a little green and gold purse.

Beth asked the shop assistant to call a taxi for her and she went back to the hotel.

"There is a message for you," said the receptionist. Would you please call this number?" She gave Beth a piece of paper.

Beth went to her room and called the number. The policeman who had taken her to the hotel answered.

"I have some news for you," he said. "Last night a motor cyclist was stopped for speeding. The rider showed the policemen a stolen driver's license - his real name was Silas Rottle. We have him in jail now. He won't bother you again."

"Thank you for telling me," said Beth.

"No problem," said the policeman. "I am sorry your first days in New Zealand were so scary. But you don't have to worry now. Please enjoy your time in New Zealand."

When Tim arrived at the hotel, Beth was waiting downstairs. She was wearing her new blue dress. Tim came into the hotel. He was wearing a dark suit.

He looks very different, thought Beth. *But he is always handsome.*

They drove to the airport in Tim's car.

"Where's the painting?" asked Beth.

"Oh, the security company is bringing it to the airport."

"Security company?"

"Yes. When I saw the picture, I knew I was right. Of course there will have to be tests done. To make sure it isn't a copy. But I think it is the real thing, and so does my boss. When I told him about it, he rushed downstairs with me to look at it. Then the rest of the day was crazy. He called a security company. He called the insurance company. He wanted a carrying box made for it. He contacted the Italians. He is very good at organizing things."

"It sounds like a lot of trouble," said Beth.

"Twelve years ago, a painting by Rubens was sold for over seventy-five million US dollars," said Tim.

"Oh," said Beth. "I understand."

At the airport, Tim drove away from the main terminal and towards a small building at the edge of the airport. "We are travelling by charter plane," he said.

There was a security van parked next to the building. Tim and Beth got out of his car and took their suitcases out of the boot.

Two men in dark suits got out of the van. They opened the back door of the van and another man climbed out. He had a chain on his wrist. The chain was attached to a wooden box with a handle.

"My boss doesn't like to take risks," said Tim laughing. "And the Italians are paying for it!"

They walked out to the charter plane. It was small jet. They climbed onto the plane with the security men. Very soon they were in the air and on their way to Wellington.

27. WELLINGTON

The plane landed at the airport in Wellington. There were two big black limousines waiting. Tim and Beth got into one car and the three security men got into the other.

They travelled into the city. The cars stopped outside a large white house in a quiet street. A man was waiting on the pavement. They followed him up to the main door of the house.

"Where are we?" asked Beth.

"It's the Italian Embassy," said Tim. "You're going to give the painting to the Ambassador."

Inside the house, they were taken to a long formal living room. The security man, who was carrying the wooden case, stopped by the door. One of the other men unlocked the chain and they put the case on a small table. They opened the case and took out the painting. They handed the painting to Beth.

"Now you are going to give it to the Ambassador," said Tim. The long room was full of people. At the far end of the room, the Ambassador was waiting behind a marble table. Beth carried the painting to the Ambassador. He bowed. She handed him the painting. He took the painting and put it on the table. He bowed again.

Several people came forward and looked at the painting. The Ambassador looked at it too. No one spoke. Then the security men came forward and the painting was put back in the box and taken away.

Then the Ambassador walked from behind the table and kissed Beth.

"Thank you!" he said. "You have returned a great treasure to us!"

Suddenly the room was very noisy. Everyone was talking and laughing. Men in white jackets appeared with trays of champagne and plates of delicious crostini. It was a very happy party.

After an hour, Tim and Beth left. They were going to meet the Ambassador and his wife for dinner. The limousine took them to a big hotel near the edge of the harbour. Beth was taken to a suite on the top floor. There was a huge bouquet of flowers in the room. The card on the flowers said, 'mille grazie'.

Beth enjoyed the hotel. She spent a long time getting dressed for dinner. Then she sat at the window of her hotel room and looked out at the harbour. It was very beautiful.

I can't believe I'm here, she thought. *It's like some crazy dream.*

Tim knocked on the door of her suite.

"Are you ready?" he asked. "We're having dinner at a restaurant near here, called Catania."

Beth picked up her little green and gold purse and put her room card in it. She joined Tim and they walked to the lift together.

"Catania?" she said. "I hope my dress isn't too formal."

"No," said Tim. "You look fabulous. I have heard of this restaurant. It is very, very good."

The limousine was waiting to take them the short distance to the restaurant.

Beth enjoyed the evening very much. The Ambassador and his wife were very friendly. The food was excellent. It was very late when they finished eating.

When the coffee was served, the Ambassador said, "I want to say something to you, Beth. Tim told me the whole story about your great-grandfather and your great-uncle. But we agreed that no one needs to know about it. Tim works with old paintings that came to New Zealand from Europe. Old paintings that were given to the museum. Often the records don't show who gave them to the museum. No one knows where they came from. We agreed that this would be the story. Tim found the Rubens inside an old picture frame in the basement of the museum. The museum gave it back to the people of Italy.

"Of course the truth is that you gave the painting back. But no one will know that. It is the only way we can protect your great-uncle's memory."

Beth smiled. "It is a very good plan, thank you."

When they left the restaurant, Tim said to Beth, "The limousine will drive us back to the hotel. But it is not so far to walk. We can walk along the edge of the water. Would you like that?"

"That sounds great," said Beth.

They walked along the edge of the harbour. Even though they were near the centre of the city, it was very quiet.

"I love it here," said Beth. "Christchurch is a perfect place to live and Wellington is great too. I think my mother would like New Zealand very much. I am going to ask her to come for a visit."

Tim stopped walking and took Beth's hands. "Does that mean you are not going back to England? Do you plan to stay here?"

"I think so," said Beth. "I have been here such a short time. But I feel like a different person. I don't want to go back to my old life. I want to stay here."

"So." Tim sounded nervous. "If I ask you to marry me, will you say yes?"

Beth laughed. She felt very, very happy. "When you ask me to marry you, I'll say yes."

THANK YOU

Thank you for reading The Legacy. (Word count: 21,974) We hope you enjoyed Beth's story.

If you would like to read more graded readers, please visit our website http://www.italkyoutalk.com

Other Level 4 graded readers include
Chi-obaa and Friends
Chi-obaa and Her Town
End House (Old Secrets – Modern Mysteries Book 2)
On the Run (Old Secrets – Modern Mysteries Book 3)
The Blue Lace Curtain (Old Secrets – Modern Mysteries Book 1)
The Witches of Nakashige
Vanished Away

ABOUT THE AUTHOR

I Talk You Talk Press is a Japan-based publisher of language textbooks, graded readers and language learning/teaching resources.

Our team is made up of highly experienced language teachers and translators, who have all studied at least one additional language to an advanced level.

This experience enables us to design our materials from the perspective of both the teacher and the learner. We consult with both teachers and language learners when designing our textbooks and graded readers, and test our materials extensively in the classroom before publication.

We are a fast-growing press, and currently publish graded readers for learners of English. We publish new graded readers monthly.

www.ingramcontent.com/pod-product-compliance
Lightning Source LLC
Chambersburg PA
CBHW032209040426
42449CB00005B/513